ACHE.
poems by zen mateo

with love. above all, with love.

rain

if my quicksand heart can develop
this near-religious level of devotion
just to streetlights reflected in the wet
pavement, how can i even begin
to discuss:

your eyes
your hand laced through mine
my name in your mouth

?

negligible senescence

today you told me that crocodiles are a little bit immortal
that if everything left them alone they would technically
never die, just grow bigger and bigger

some kinds of feelings are like crocodiles and why do we
always think of eternal love as something soft?
some loves are rough-scaled and sharp-toothed and
all-consuming in a very literal kind of way

some loves, if left alone, will just relentlessly keep existing
will just lurk in marshy waters, growing and growing
some loves have no natural predators
except starvation and disease

and maybe she's your forever love
and maybe i'll always blush when i hear your name

muscle memory

life goes dark your lips on mine and our hands
shift like tectonic plates at the beginning of time
fingers through your hair our bodies together
a landscape encompassing everything.

softhardwetdrysmoothrough
hills and valleys and rivers,
waterfalls i will spend my life chasing goddamnit

the sky in your eyes, the ocean in my mouth.

habits

i can taste you
on my teeth
i am usually scared
of drugs as hard as you

ex-boyfriend

i think of you when my heart skips beats (which sounds poetic but really i'm supposed to see a doctor; young hearts aren't meant to flutter like that) i think of you when i'm slurring my words, when my hands shake so much i can't hold a pen. i think of you, in other words, when i'm on the brink. the only time i think of holding your hand is when trains hurtle toward me and i have to press my back against the far wall of the subway platform for fear of -

yours is still a name i wake up saying, but only from nightmares.

honey

maybe i am so often quiet because i am afraid
that my words could turn out to have sharp edges
and scratch your throat when you swallow them
when what you deserve is sweetness, softness,
the sticky promise that i will never fail to water
the blossoms in your soul

you shouldn't have to be brave with me.
flowers should not have to explain.

fi

i like your soft laugh in the dark,
a piece of the night sky.

depression

there's nothing cute about it
nothing poetic
in not washing my hair for four days
nothing tragically beautiful
about the blood on my shaky hands
there is nothing desirable
about the way the color
is wrung out of your vision
gradually,
and then all at once.

but i understand why you might think this way.

i too have been enchanted by fire,
by the flickering, brilliant flames
i too have forgotten to consider
that which is being consumed

mama

i have heard that a
finish-each-other's-sentences kind of love
is rare to find.

but in our case, of course it makes sense.
we have been completing each other's heartbeats
since the dark water when i was only a soul.

dad

quiet freeway friend to my heart
you have taught me how to love loud.
how to love in overflowing bags of goldfish crackers
and entire plastic supermarket baskets of raspberries
and all the colors of your paint-smeared hands to love
in songs and laughter and all the cash in my wallet
to love with every ounce of this vivid heart

sister

what runs deeper -
the magma at the core of the earth,
or my instinct to call out to you?
(on sleepless nights, in crowded rooms,
from the backs of runaway horses)

your heart is as big as the pacific
and your love will bring the kind of
powerful, briny, shiny, kelp-filled
catharsis
this world needs

brother

brother of mine you have always
walked into our dark empty house
ahead of me, ready to lunge
at anything that could be lurking.

did you know that i am equally ready
to fight for you and for your softness,
for your humid rainforest heart,
for the flowers blooming in your ribcage

?

(never forget how deeply i love
the gentle green music of your soul)

september

blue is bluer than blue tonight,
colors are the kind of vivid
that i used to think
came only with falling in love.

girly

look at how the sky is reflected
in your manicured fingernails.
look at how infinity can in exist
in such a small, polished surface area.

abyss

i sit down on the steps at lincoln center,
and i begin to cry.
what does it mean to be still
in the middle of all this aching, chaotic beauty?
sometimes, a city is as good as an ocean.
as infinite, as vast, as good at reminding me
that i am miniscule.
i lie down on my back and stare up at the sky.
night is falling fast, as if it is heavy,
as if it has been thrown down, hard,
from a great height.

house party

a strange kind of person who can scald your temperate blood,
can make you want to go outside and scream at the hudson river
(you who drink your own anger like cheap vodka you whose voice
is so soft you're never not repeating yourself)

a strange kind of person who can make an entire room full of
beating hearts meaningless can make you reach for a
curling iron and a knife in the same night

can make you remember lines of spanish poetry
when you're drunk out of your mind –

last night someone told me that i'm so beautiful i don't even
look human. which is bizarre but also, i think, fitting.
i don't feel very human these days.

and also, what is the point of a beauty
that can't pull you to me from one block away?

instinct

i want to have
a daughter
with dark curls and
with a loud voice and
with impossibly sweet little
pudgy hands

instinct ii

i will have a daughter
and name her Brave.

kinds of privilege

i was born with a silver spoon, full
of mango sorbet and my father's poetry
a mouth full of cool sweetness
and soft words of love
full before i even opened my eyes
i swallowed before i drew my first breath

baby of the family, sunshine girl

i was born on my due date
at noon on a saturday
my mother's easiest labor
born at home, in the springtime
i came softly into light and love

high school boyfriends

you never left me alone with my darkness
when my heart beat too fast, you held me to yours
i can never repay you

megan

but somehow,
i felt lighter in her slender, perfect arms
than i ever did in any boy's

beautiful i

to be called beautiful
is always a relief
because it reminds me that
despite life
certain things remain constant

beautiful ii

beautiful, he says,
and i drink the wonder in his eyes

beautiful iii

beautiful, she says,
leaning over to whisper in my ear
and i laugh because
i am not a mirror

beautiful iv

beautiful, the artist says,
looking into my face
like it's an ocean
gentle, the artist says, with a bite.
sweet-hot, like red chili sauce

beautiful v

at the store, buying conditioner/walking down the street in my
sweaty dance clothes/ordering a coffee, yawning absurdly, in my
own world

"so beautiful."

who is he? how long has he been watching me?

and i am pulled,
abruptly,
by my eyelashes,
back into the reality of objecthood.

beautiful vi

sometimes beauty feels like a wall
i sit behind it and lean my head
against the cool stone surface
hiding, waiting, protecting myself

genesis

and you know i didn't used to believe
that god made the first woman from somebody else's rib
but that might explain why, even after everything,
i am still drawn to sleep on your chest.
why our synchronized breathing still feels like something sacred

it's not to say that i'm not also made from stardust
but somewhere, mixed in with all that infinity,
maybe there lives a piece of you.
maybe it aches for you when you're far from me
and maybe that's what really splinters when i feel my heart break

ex-lover

i tried to shake you out of my heart
like sand out of a beach towel.
but still i find traces of you,
glittery and abrasive;
in my shoes, my hair,
my shower, my sheets.
you're everywhere.
you are still everywhere.

evidence

somewhere
in the darkness before i had fingernails,
my soul knew things.

philosophy

i am not an abstract concept.
find me in the air that stirs
as i leap across the studio,
listen for me
in the cascading sound of my laughter,
feel for the essence of my existence
in the curve of my hips.
discover my infinite actuality
trapped in my eyelashes like snowflakes.

sonnet i

my ballet teacher finishes giving a combination at the barre,
and then asks when in the music
we should turn around and start the other side.
count 7, someone offers.
start the turn on seven, so you're around by 8
and can start the second side on 1.
count 8, someone else suggests, turn around on 8,
it's just half a turn and you don't need that much time.
it turns out we were all wrong.
you should turn around in the space between 8 and 1.

i want to exist with you in the liminal space between 8 and 1.
i want to cuddle into this compact little eternity.
i want you to kiss me in that way that makes everything else fall
away, that way that makes it feel like my soul is shedding its skin.

art school

and what a blessing it is to be going to class
so i can learn how to push my soul out through my chest,
how to spit my heart out into my hand
and offer it to the person in front of me.
how amazing is it that my
nine-to-five-school-supplies-bread-and-peanut-butter-
get-out-of-bed-for-this reality
is the connection to the deepest rivers of myself,
the living, breathing poetry of the universe.
is there any better life than this?

on being a dancer

and for this, i would
swallow a lit match
every morning

music theory

she explains that the first note of a scale
is called the tonic
and that all the other notes in a piece played in that key
will gravitate toward it.
i start tearing up at my desk, because this is what love is.
finding that person who is eternally tonic.
(drown yourself in gin, but this is chronic)
no matter where else you go,
you will always be pulled back,
be it soft and dreamy or kicking and screaming;
back to this sound because,
without it -

crush

and you hit me
like a storm, no
you hit me like
an entire season unto yourself

astronomy

krishna's mother knew he was a god because
she looked in his mouth and she saw the universe.

this is why kissing is a big deal.
because you never know
when you will be pressed up against the wall
at some party
and you stick your tongue in someone's mouth
and suddenly you taste creation.

you taste the sea and the mountains and the sky
and all the stars
and you were just looking for a night out
looking to blow off some steam,
but instead you have tasted eternity.
and maybe you weren't ready for that and

you are not the only person
who has ever spat stars into my unsuspecting mouth
but i think maybe yours burned me
the brightest.

peyton

i don't think i am okay enough
to pull you up and out of this,
so maybe just drag me down.
just in terms of physics,
i think that's the way to go.
i'd rather not have to
stop holding your hand.

ambiguous

you wonder, always,
and you don't wonder, ever,
because you already know,

why telling a white girl she's beautiful
ends with the word beautiful,
and a period.

and telling a girl like you
that she's beautiful never does.

it ends with

what

are

you

and a question mark

sonnet ii

last night i had a dream
that the pain in my legs
rose up through my flesh
in the form of
painted flowers on my skin.
and i went to the doctor
and he said,
"i have never seen a case this severe."
it was unsettling,
partly because of the idea of something
rising up through me like that,
but mostly because

i didn't care about the pain.
i just cared about the beauty.

schema

my mother is a midwife. when i was a little girl she explained to me about cesarean sections, or c-sections, as they are sometimes called. she told me about how sometimes, it is not possible for the baby to safely come out of the mother in the usual way, so they have to cut open the mother's belly. but whenever she mentioned this, for some reason i imagined the term in my head not as c-section with the letter c, but as sea, s-e-a-section. i imagined my mama cutting open a woman's belly and finding the baby swimming in ocean water, with the kelp and the waves and the sparkling gold specks.

to some extent, i think i still believe this. i believe that inside every person, inside women especially, is the ocean. that everyone i pass on the street carries a salty, wavy infinity in their belly.

ally

i have grown to understand
that the kind of
being brown in America
that i am
is a different kind.

it's a slinky kind.
it is a
doe-eyed
lotus blossom
ethnic princess
hey girl you're so exotic
kind.

it is not a
fear for my life
every time
i leave the house
kind.

it is not a
burned and
whipped and
chained
into my blood memory
kind.

casual

you have somehow sidled
into my sticky, wide-open heart,
you lanky, ridiculous miracle,
and you're refusing to leave.

i remember the first time i ever saw you
(luminous, cosmic, unbelievable)

i didn't even realize we had something that could end
but based on the current state of my heart...

over you

after all, you are
no kind of home
for my soul

friday

the NYPD broke down
your neighbor's door this morning.
i imagine you curled in your bed,
shaking.
this shouldn't happen to you.
i hate everything about this.
you tell me you'll recover
and that you just won't go to class today.

i wish i could wrap my
stupid delicate self
around you,
shield you from everything.
i was not made to fight,
but i'd fight anyone who hurt you.
i was born a soft compact ocean,
but surely for you i could be a wildfire

stoic

and do you ever feel like
you have to physically hold your life together,
cling wildly onto the pieces
by your chipped-polish fingernails,
because through the cracks and tears
in your everyday life,
you can see
the entire vivid aching universe
shining through?

ever since

things that scare me:

-hands that inevitably slide up my skirt
-kisses that turn hungry
-having to explain
-the nights

new york

this city is humanity's night light,
that pulsing, ever-present glow
that reminds you that
everything will be okay.
this city stays up all night
so you don't have to.

chemistry

this one goes out to all my girls
all my girls who cling to each other
through the nights, clasping hands
against the emptiness praying
that our souls aren't soluble in
blood, smoke, vodka, stomach acid, or tears

tolerance

people say i'm a lightweight, but darling
i could take you like shots of tequila, even without the lime.
i could drink you from a straw like my first vodka cranberry
from a real live bartender in the downtown club
where girls like me get in for free
i could drink you after you after you after you
from flimsy plastic waiting room cups on a rooftop
like the cheapest rum i've ever encountered
i could just upend a handle of you into my mouth and stop
breathing i could roll you and light you and smoke you like
strange expensive east coast weed i could drink cases and
bottles and cups and shots and glasses
and mouthfuls and oceans and
seas and galaxies
of you

and i would still walk in a straight line up 9th avenue
all the way home

impression

you know how sometimes
someone kisses you and
you taste it for weeks

and it's like cotton candy in slow motion

theology

you know when someone
has the kind of eyes
that serve as evidence
for the existence of god

(because someone must have made you
certain things i can believe are random.
you, no)

they say that miracles
are only real to those
who experience them firsthand
in other words, let me hold you.

spring

you asked,
don't you need an umbrella?
and i told you,
i'm not made of sugar.
and you asked,
are you sure about that?

serina

darling, you and i can never be pulled apart.
we grew up on oceans of the same blues.

tech week

it is as if when you were here
i asked for to someone spike you
to outline your being in glow tape
on the dusty floor of my heart
so i could find the place you belong
even in the blackout.

alex

it is of course about the words
that we say at the same time
and the things that are only funny to us
but even more, it's about
the silences we inhabit together,
the way my soul reaches out to yours
like sunflowers turning to the light,
comfortable and urgent,
soft-yellow and infinite,
like the first step into a heated room

i'm sorry

i know that you have third degree burns
from the light in my eyes

affirmations

even champagne bubbles
cast a shadow,
even the moon
goes dark sometimes,
diamonds
can slice your skin open,
oysters form pearls
as a coping mechanism,
palm trees
survive hurricanes,
and maybe i am strong enough for this

winter

beware of windows, of frank ocean,
of flower shops and sunsets and
tall strangers in denim jackets,
beware of the butterfly
at the base of your throat
that somehow still knows his name.

how would you set a trap for an angel?

originally, when someone said this, the idea that came to me was something to do with all the random, unexpected, aggressively-not-angelic things i could use to set traps for you, you know, hennessy, weed, strange salty foods like foods like crab and ritz crackers, tongue piercings, horror movies, aliens, knives.

but there are two problems with this. one is that for every example i could use to fill this narrative, there are infinite things about you that are as archetypically angelic as it gets. violets, peonies, perfume, sparkling wine, soft blankets, music, love poems, peaches, rain.

and the other is that in my heart of hearts i know
that if angels are real, i want them to be free.

wednesday

i feel it most on days like today
(a reaching out from the center of me)
even if i know all you would say
is you love me
and "you're lovely"
and you'll fix my heart as best you can and
you really just wish you could hold me

you were never really mine but that didn't stop my heart
from growing violet-flowered vines that wrapped themselves,
tightly, around the idea of you, or maybe, if i'm honest, us.

sensitive

do you ever feel like maybe your heart
is made of porcelain or choux pastry?
like something about it is just destined
to shatter and crumble and fall apart?

and do you ever feel like maybe your soul
is so vast and liquid and salty that
you could probably drown
in your own throat?

sweetheart

i think sometimes people forget
that a thing can be so sweet it hurts you.

if you hold my heart in your mouth for too long,
it could rot your teeth.

it could spike your blood sugar,
bring you crashing down,
shaky, unsteady,

and somehow emptier than you were before.

linguistics

don't you think there should be
a separate grammatical tense
for people you have loved?

sisa

as far as i know
the inside of you is
three dimensional,
it's like
installation art
or, if it's a book,
it's a pop up book.

slowly

i am trying to believe
that my tendency to love
like most people breathe
is a strength
rather than a weakness,
because maybe
life can only be miraculous
if you are relentlessly open
to the idea of miracles.

old love

i think that to you,
i was always beautiful
in the way of
a small and wild creature,
a little prosecco hurricane,
and not, for instance,
in the way of an ocean.

mirage

girls like you are not interested in my love
you are interested in
my lipstick mark on the edge of a coffee mug
my visible breath in the cold air
the way my name tastes in your mouth
(especially when you're using it
to chase shots of liquor, a sugar-sweet
afterthought
easy going down)
what my hair looks like from far away and
most importantly
the way the abstract idea of me makes
your current girlfriend's breath
catch in her throat.

word choice

i prefer the word delicate.
because it is similar to the word fragile,
but without the implied shattering.
something that is fragile is in a sense
destined to be broken
but something that is delicate
can just be.

thursday meditations

soft smiling men on the subway
with hands like my father's.
the idea that all there is is change, and also:
what you thought was the floor of my heart
is really a trap door.

eating disorder

i want to scrape out my stomach with a spatula, calmly slide the contents off its edge with one finger, and repeat until the inside of me is bitter and light. until i am a paper lantern, thin layers folded in on themselves, lit from the inside, floating.

i want to poke holes in the bottoms of feet and let everything drain out of me like water through a sieve, until nothing remains but my skeleton, bones smooth like mahjong tiles cream colored and clicky and set out to dry in the sun.

if this were about beauty i could have stopped long ago. i want to disappear. i want to sandpaper all the softness off my frame. softness invites kisses and knives but i want to be hard as driftwood. storm-tossed and hollow.

would that i could be nothing but wide eyes and sharp teeth.

yes

it is okay
to bury your fears

but not in the way
you bury something dead

bury them in the way
you bury treasure

or, even better,
in the way you bury seeds.

process

images rise like acid in my mouth and there's nowhere to spit them out so i just swallow. every day for six months fire down my throat, flames licking my ribcage, and no one knows. she's out there subway stations and classrooms and hallways out there coffee and toast out there smiling/laughing out there growing/thriving out there friends with my friends out there having stolen the light behind my eyes *and no one knows.* six months later, me, topless in a chilly doctor's office, watching black and white images of my heart move on a screen, trying to read the expression in my mother's eyes to determine if she's worried. the nurse turns to me and says, *now this angle is as if your heart was an orange, and i have cut it in half.* i think to myself, my heart *was* an orange, a summer-sweet tangerine, and someone has already sliced it up and sucked it dry. she adjusts the settings on the echocardiogram so that i can hear the sound of my heart beating. it is much wetter than you would think, flowing ocean water and tangerine juice and nervous, choking-hazard tears.

to the woman who assaulted me

will you ever know how much it hurts
to want to kill the parts of you that sparkle?

post-traumatic

i woke up drowning
in a specific kind of sadness.
a morning-after-a-breakup
kind of sadness
a missing-your-first-love
kind of sadness
and i was mystified,
until i realized that
the person i miss is myself.
i miss the me i used to be.
i am homesick for the self
before all this happened
(the self i felt safe with)
i ache for her.

in der nacht

i was up all night talking to you,
curled around my phone on speaker,
waiting for your voice to turn to honey.
it took two hours, but it happened.
your words turned soft and sweet and
just for me and the velvety dark world
outside my window turned
into an extended elaborate inside joke
between us and i felt my own voice
soften in my throat, syllables tripping
lithely over each other,
spilling from my lips like peach juice and

calling you baby again felt like coming up for air.

why are you avoiding me?

i know that i have a tendency to shatter, and i don't want the sharp pieces to cut your perfect hands; i have been down this road far too many times with far too many bright eyed people.

how to survive a mother who is also a wildfire

one. cut fire lines. clear out all the flammable material from the fire's path. contain it.

two. where possible, set your own fires. periodically setting controlled burns will make it so that the wildfire won't be able to do as much damage.

three. keep your mouth closed so you don't inhale smoke.

four. always touch doors with the backs of your hands before trying to open them.

five. at a certain point, water won't help.

six. break your window and jump out.

seven. take nothing with you. run.

eight. return (never alone) only after it is safe.

nine. watch out for hot spots and loose ash; even after a fire has been extinguished, small fires can flare up without warning.

ten. be sure to document all damage.

fi ii

you made the sky glow orange
and the night go soft and silent.
you turned my twin bed
into a warm moonlit ocean
i don't really sleep anymore,
but with you here that's somehow okay.
your hair smells like rain,
and when i woke up this morning
i thought i heard birds singing.

since when are there birds in this city?

safe

i keep thinking i'm safe because this world doesn't want to kill me
thinking i'm safe because san diego doesn't really have trains to
jump in front of or because the windows in my new york
apartment are painted shut and i don't have a bathtub to bleed
out in, only a tiny shower full of cherry blossom conditioner and
lavender soap and pink handled razors that…well. i guess aren't
that safe after all but still. thinking i'm safe because i have a
phone smart enough to call an alexa brave enough to clean up
the blood thin enough to run for what feels like an hour and
thinking i'm safe because i have translucent child locked bottles
of blue pills and a team of calm, serious people with steady
hands trying to determine what percent of me is made of china
and if it really makes sense for me to be kept in such high places
all the time, thinking i'm safe because straight vodka on an empty
stomach won't kill you in your sleep if you never go to sleep
thinking that the stars in my eyes won't burn me up from the
inside because by the time you see them stars are already dead
because any sea monster that has taken up residence deep in
the center of me will soon be starved or smoked or acid-burned
out and do you see a problem here?

hapa

my father recently told me that for him,
calling me hapa isn't about
me being half white.

it's about me being his half-moon moonlight,
half himself and half the love of his life,
his hope for the future,
his glass half full.

by pure coincidence, the day
he married my mother
was an anniversary
of the day he came to this country.

and all of this is to say
that i can stop believing in light
and in life and in my own heart beating,
but i will never stop believing in love.

to the flowers growing on my windowsill

at first i thought there was something wrong with you
why are you bending and leaning like that?
but then i realized
(quiet, ecstatic, unbelievably blessed)
that you are just reaching toward the light.

days/daze

days like
days when you
days when i want to get on the treadmill, crank it up to 10.5, and
stop running. just let it hurl me backwards shattered mirror pieces
through the abyss.
days like
days when you
days when my wrists itch and i know that there are whispery
ghosts and impatient creatures in my watery blood
days like
days when you
days when i just want to throw myself out the window, off a cliff,
spread my arms and open my mouth and drink the sky i've read
days like
days when
days and
i've heard
that i'd be dead before i even hit the ground.

an epiphany

something that is immensely comforting to me
on days like today
is the fact that my heart
is a muscle.

and muscles can hurt like hell,
but they can't break.

my heart can be sore, strained, sprained, torn
it can spasm and it can ache and it can
get so tired it's shaking uncontrollably.

but it can't break, and at the end of the day,

i'm a dancer.
i know how to deal with a sore muscle.

i can heat it and roll it out with a lacrosse ball and i can
stretch it and rub tiger balm on it and i can
give it a rest from certain movements and my heart
can hurt like fucking hell.
but it cannot ever break.

and also, even more miraculously,
the pain can mean it's getting stronger.

resonance

i may be
a hollow shell of a person
these days,
but even if that's true,
at least know this:
i am the kind of hollow shell
that when you lift me to your ear,
you can hear the ocean.

things i have inherited from my mother

broad shoulders,
resilience,
a sweet tooth,
the ability to burn sage and start again
(any number of times)
courage to walk the labyrinth,
sparkly eyes, and above all,
a voice from somewhere deep,
saying, always:
you are enough

always

did you not read the poems i wrote about you?
you write poems about everything
not like this.

flow

you make me feel dumb things i'm talking like
frank sinatra things
soft slow songs late night unexpected harmonies
pinching myself because you can't be like this
and be real and be looking back at me
like that.
those kinds of things i swear to god

you make me feel dumb things yo i'm talking
wild sweet things swinging laced together
hands too lucky to be mine down ninety sixth street
air too sweet to be april you make me feel -
amy winehouse straight tequila on an empty stomach
things. steamy uptown parties and not enough air
for all these lungs baby you know i'm no good
i'll never be any good especially not for you
and still you make me feel -

you know the kind of days you want to
pour into a chilled glass and sip forever?

slice

blood is cold and wet and
i am not allowed to start fires
but if i were -

a long time ago, doctors
used to cut open sick people
so that the bad could flow out

i wonder why they stopped.

parents

thank you for believing that
the wild gardens of my heart
are worth watering
thank you for believing that
my voice is worth listening to
even if it's soft and shaky
thank you for imagining
this highly colored life for me

construction

rickety scaffolding
hung with strings of lights,
which is to say
this is temporary
but that doesn't make it
undeserving of its beauty.

origins

once i dreamt that the world was
smooth and blank and my father,
a painter,
was the one who added the colors.

two hands

two hands, zen.

me, as a little girl, carrying something
that my parents wanted me to be careful with.

two hands, zen.

after today, after whatever it was
that turned your eyes green like your name   .
after today, i know this:

whatever we have, darling,
i'm going to carry it with two hands.

not because i'm worried it's going to break.
but because i think it might contain something
that could spill.

(probably something like the soup you're
never not eating, something warm and
splashy and ridiculous)

two hands, zen.
two hands, yours and mine?
two hands, sweets, it's very full.

eden

be careful about building walls.
do not forget that god is a gardener.

that god has
warm, callused,
clay-brown hands.

that creating the world every day
requires backbreaking labor.

depression ii / this is not about you

how could you
expect
a drowning woman
to explain to you
the nature of the ocean
the concept of salt water
the scrape of sand in her lungs
how much she misses
air
?

radiant

warm and enchanting
as if you have
swallowed the sun
yet remain unscathed

x

remember glowsticks?
you snap them
and they light up.

the next person who loves me

needs to love me blind needs to love me standing still love me in the dark love me broken love me silent love me messy and mad and finding my voice love me powerful love me like an equal love me brave and love me small love me rough around the edges screw it love me rough all the way through to the center of me love me love me crawling toward somewhere that isn't here love me rooted like a tree love me fast and slow and love me like you love your own heart beating love me like your first breath and your last love me pure and love me vital love me real love me deep and love me sure love me like the answer to a question you've been asking for years and like a question to an answer you been holding forever love me with your entire self love me even if i had no eyelashes or even no eyes at all love me like the center of something and like the edges of it too love me run on sentences love me a song that shakes your soul love me clear running water love me a wave too big for you but you've already caught it, my dude, love me in slow motion love me at the top of your lungs love me six shots of tequila love me a hole you punched in the wall love me far from home love me calm love me certain love me love me all your eggs in one beat up basket love me like it's the only thing you have left to do in this life.

anxiety

thoughts chase each other
around my head like bright fish
in a too-small tank

salt water sloshes from my eyes.

firefly

you once said that you wished
you could be a raindrop.
but if you were a raindrop,
you would not hear me
when i say i love you.
if you were a raindrop
i could not hold your hand.

dream

it takes a goddess with
translucent wrists and
breakable veins to create
a world capable of bleeding
like this

something i have learned

try not to put yourself into any boxes
it is hard to breathe inside a box.

zen mateo is a twenty-year-old artist from san diego, california. she currently lives in new york city, where she is pursuing a bfa in dance at the alvin ailey school.

Made in the USA
Middletown, DE
19 October 2017